Philip Ridley

Tende

Five poems from

Lovesongs for ...res

Methuen Drama

Published by Methuen Drama 2011

Methuen Drama, an imprint of Bloomsbury Publishing Plc

1 3 5 7 9 10 8 6 4 2

Methuen Drama
Bloomsbury Publishing Plc
36 Soho Square
London W1D 3QY
www.methuendrama.com

First published by Methuen Drama in 2011

Copyright © Philip Ridley 2011

The author has asserted his rights under the Copyright, Designs
and Patents Act 1988 to be identified as the author of this work.

ISBN: 978 1 408 15287 4

A CIP catalogue record for this book is available from the British Library

Available in the USA from Bloomsbury Academic & Professional, 175 Fifth
Avenue/3rd Floor, New York, NY 10010. www.BloomsburyAcademicUSA.com

Typeset by Mark Heslington Ltd, Scarborough, North Yorkshire
Printed and bound in Great Britain by CPI Cox & Wyman, Reading, RG1 8EX

Caution

Ben Monks and Will Young for

supporting wall

present

Tender Napalm
by Philip Ridley

World Premiere at Southwark Playhouse, London,
on Tuesday 19 April 2011

Tender Napalm
by Philip Ridley

Cast

MAN   Jack Gordon
WOMAN   Vinette Robinson

Director	David Mercatali
Set & lighting designer	William Reynolds
Music by	Nick Bicât
Movement director	Tom Godwin
Stage manager	Julia Blom
Assistant director	Kay Michael
Produced by	Ben Monks & Will Young for Supporting Wall

Production supported by the Kobler Trust. With thanks to Naima Khan at Spoonfed, Ajay Jayaram at Cable, Liam Welton at Chaotic Creations, Charlotte Loveridge at Methuen Drama, Nicholas Allott at Cameron Mackintosh, Thelma Holt and Stephen Waley-Cohen.

Presented by kind permission of the Rod Hall Agency Limited of Lower Ground Floor, 7 Mallow Street, London EC1Y 8RQ.

Supporting Wall Limited is a not for profit company registered in England and Wales, number 7081594.

www.supportingwall.com

Philip Ridley

Philip was born in the East End of London where he still lives and works. He studied painting at St Martin's School of Art and his work has been exhibited widely throughout Europe and Japan. As well as three books for adults and the highly acclaimed screenplay for *The Krays* (winner of the *Evening Standard* Best Film of the Year Award), he has written seven adult stage plays: *The Pitchfork Disney*, the multi-award-winning *The Fastest Clock in the Universe*, *Ghost from a Perfect Place*, *Vincent River*, the controversial *Mercury Fur*, *Leaves of Glass* and *Piranha Heights*, plus several plays for young people: *Karamazoo*, *Fairytaleheart*, *Sparkleshark*, *Brokenville* and *Moonfleece*.

He has also written many books for children, including *Scribbleboy* (shortlisted for the Carnegie Medal), *Kasper in the Glitter* (nominated for the Whitbread Prize), *Mighty Fizz Chilla* (shortlisted for the Blue Peter Book of the Year Award), *ZinderZunder*, *Vinegar Street*, *Zip's Apollo* and the bestseller *Krindlekrax* (winner of both the Smarties Prize and WH Smith's Mind-Boggling Books Award), the stage play of which – adapted by Philip himself – was premiered at the Birmingham Rep Theatre in the summer of 2002.

Philip has also directed three feature films from his own screenplays: *The Reflecting Skin*, winner of eleven international awards including the prestigious George Sadoul Prize; *The Passion of Darkly Noon*, winner of the Best Director Prize at the Porto Film Festival; and most recently *Heartless*, winner of The Silver Meliers Award for Best Fantasy Film and starring Jim Sturgess and Noel Clarke, released in May 2010. He has also recently written his first opera libretto, *Tarantula In Petrol Blue*, premiered at Aldeburgh, with music by Anna Meredith.

Philip has won both the *Evening Standard*'s Most Promising Newcomer to British Film and Most Promising Playwright Awards – the only person ever to receive both prizes.

Jack Gordon

Jack trained at RADA and was named one of the 2010 *Screen International* UK Stars of Tomorrow.

Jack's stage credits include *War Horse*, *DNA* and *The Miracle* at the National Theatre; *Lulu* and *The Car Cemetery* at the Gate; and the role of Romeo in Polly Findlay's JMK Award-winning production of *Romeo and Juliet* at the Battersea Arts Centre.

Jack's film work includes Philip Ridley's *Heartless*, Andrea Arnold's *Fish Tank*, Gurinder Chadha's *It's A Wonderful Afterlife*, Sean Hogan's *The Devil's Business*, Joe Johnston's Marvel Studios epic *Captain America*, Chris Crow's *Panic Button*, Robert Heath's *Truth or Dare* and Alex Barrett's *Life Just Is*.

Television work includes *Law & Order: UK*, *EastEnders*, *The Bill*, *Primeval* and *Lewis*.

Vinette Robinson

Vinette trained at Webber Douglas, where she won a Laurence Olivier Bursary; and she first came to attention for a small role in Mike Leigh's film *Vera Drake*. Other film credits include *Imagine Me & You* and *Powder*.

Vinette's stage credits include *Welcome to Thebes* and *Measure for Measure* at the National Theatre; *Darker Shores* at the Hampstead Theatre; Shared Experience's *War and Peace*; Headlong Theatre's *Paradise Lost*; *Sugar Mummies* at the Royal Court; and *Speaking Like Magpies*, *Sejanus*, *A New Way to Please You* and *Thomas Moore*, all for the RSC.

Her most recent television work includes the series regular DS Sally Donovan in the BBC drama *Sherlock*, returning for a second season later this year. Other TV credits include roles in *Waterloo Road*, *The Passion* and *Party Animals*.

David Mercatali

David is a director and writer based in London. Recent directing credits include the acclaimed and controversial 2010 professional premiere production of Philip Ridley's *Moonfleece*; *Weights* at the Blue Elephant Theatre; *Runners: The Return* at Underbelly (Edinburgh Festival); and *People's Day* at the Pleasance Islington.

David's first play, *The Sound*, premiered in 2009 at the Blue Elephant Theatre to critical acclaim.

David was Assistant Director on *The Eleventh Capital* at the Royal Court Theatre and has developed new work at the Southwark Playhouse and Oval House Theatre among others. He is currently working on a verbatim theatre piece, *Someone to Blame*, developed at Theatre 503.

William Reynolds

William Reynolds trained at the Motley Theatre Design School. Recent set and lighting designs include *Waiting* (Southbank Centre), *Otieno*, *Blood Wedding* (both Southwark Playhouse), *Saturday Night* (Arts Theatre), *Moonfleece* (London & UK Tour) and *La Boheme* (Choir of London Palestine Tour).

Lighting includes *Daredevas* (Southbank Centre), *Nuit d'Electronique et d'Opera* (Theatre Royal de Wallonie, Belgium), *The Magic Flute* (Choir of London Palestine Tour), *The Company Man* (Orange Tree Theatre), *Black-i* (Oval House Theatre) and *Pulse* (The Place).

Projection designs include *Prima Donna* (Sadler's Wells), *The Gambler* (Royal Opera House), *Das Rheingold* (Nationale Reisopera, Holland) and *Home* (Theatre Royal Bath).

Nick Bicât

Nick is a composer whose work ranges from mass-audience television to art-house cinema and theatre. He has twice been nominated for a BAFTA, for *Cruel Train* and *Holding On*.

Nick has a long-standing feature film collaboration with Philip Ridley, most recently writing an album of eleven songs for *Heartless* (to lyrics by Ridley himself). His score for Ridley's *The Passion Of Darkly Noon* won the award for Best Music Score at the 1995 Film Festival in Sitges, Barcelona, and the theme song 'Who Will Love Me Now?' (Bicât/Ridley) was sung by PJ Harvey and achieved popular success as a single.

Nick's extensive theatrical work includes original scores for the National Theatre (including *Pravda* and *King Lear*) and RSC (*The Greeks*). His opera *The Knife* (book & lyrics by David Hare and Tim Rose-Price) was nominated for the New York Drama Desk Award for Best Musical Score.

He is currently working on more songs with Ridley and scoring a major public event on Rutland Water in June 2011.

Tom Godwin

Tom trained at Ecole Jacques Lecoq.

Movement direction includes *Get Santa* at the Royal Court, *Earthquakes in London* at the National Theatre, *Victory* at the Arcola, *Restoration* at the Salisbury Playhouse and *Lucky You* at Oxford Playhouse and Assembly Rooms Edinburgh.

Recent acting credits include *Get Santa* at the Royal Court, *Earthquakes in London* at the National Theatre and *ENRON* at the Minerva Theatre Chichester, the Royal Court and in the West End.

Julia Blom

Julia has a background in event and project management in the Netherlands. In London she has worked at Sadler's Wells and the Barbican, and she has been a Venue Stage Manager for Pleasance Edinburgh for the last two years. Julia's stage management credits include *Macbeth* (Broadway Theatre), *Miss Julie* (Arcola Theatre), *Sister Of* (Nursery Festival), *Secret Boulevard* (Courtyard Theatre), *MEAT* (The Albany & Lion and Unicorn), *Oh, To Be in England* (Finborough Theatre) and *Fragments* (Riverside Studios). She has also worked on several festivals at the Royal Albert Hall and Sadler's Wells, including *Breakin' Convention 09* and *10*.

Kay Michael

Kay studied at Warwick University, where she gained a First Class degree in English and Theatre Studies, and has since directed Bernie Shevlin's *The Nth Degree* at the Off Cut Festival (Old Red Lion Theatre) and the Branching Out Festival (Rosemary Branch Theatre); directed for two seasons of new writing at the Oval House Theatre; and worked with Philip Ridley on an independent site-specific promenade production of *Mercury Fur*. She directs and devises work with Curious Directive, of which she is a founding member. Assistant directing credits also include *Return to the Silence* (Pleasance Theatre, Islington) and *Othello* (Lauderdale House).

Supporting Wall

Producing company Supporting Wall was founded in 2008 by Ben Monks and Will Young. *Tender Napalm* is their second collaboration with Philip Ridley, following their acclaimed and controversial professional premiere of *Moonfleece*, in London and on UK tour in the run-up to the 2010 General Election.

Other Supporting Wall productions in 2010 – a year for which they received a Best Producer nomination at the OffWestEnd 'Offie' Awards – include the JMK Award-winning production of *The Jewish Wife* at the Battersea Arts Centre (also longlisted for the Offie Awards for Best Direction, Best Design and Best Actress) and the rapid-response political theatre event *Election Drama* at the New Players Theatre. The latter was described by the *New Statesman* as 'a breathtaking feat of theatrical chutzpah'.

Other productions to date include a mini-series of American writing at the Finborough Theatre, a devised show for children touring London and the south east, and a co-production with Theatre Ad Infinitum at the 2009 Edinburgh Festival of *Odyssey*, winner of the *Stage* Award for Best Solo Performance. Supporting Wall has also managed and promoted UK and international tours for a range of clients.

In June 2009, Ben and Will were awarded the SOLT/TMA Stage One Bursary for New Producers to pursue their work with Supporting Wall, and they remain grateful for this support as well as the assistance of many individuals and organisations who have made their work possible.

For more information, visit www.supportingwall.com.

Tender Napalm

*Sexual love is the most stupendous fact
of the universe and the most magical mystery
our poor blind senses know.*
Amy Lowell

*We must embrace pain and burn it
as fuel for our journey.*
Kenji Miyazawa

Our life is what our thoughts make it.
Marcus Aurelius

Characters

Man
Woman

Man Your mouth.

Woman What about it?

Man It's such a . . . wet thing.

Slight pause.

I could squeeze a bullet between those lips. Point first.
Press it between those rosebud lips. Prise it between your
pearly whites. Gently. I wouldn't break a single tooth. Your
tongue would feel something cold and hard. Taste of metal
and gunpowder. There might even be a slight . . . retching
reflex. I'd wait a moment. I'd make calming, soothing
noises. I'd be like a . . . like a tree full of doves spreading my
cooing branches around you. Then . . . then I'd continue
pushing slowly, so slowly. You'd be quite calm by now. Your
mouth would relax. You would accept this bullet in your
palette. It would feel as natural as . . . as a pearl in the palm
of an oyster.

Woman   . . . You're in a fucking poetic mood.

Man It's all your fault.

Woman Me?

Man You . . . inspire me.

Woman Oh, my love.

Man My love.

Slight pause.

Woman Your eyes.

Man What about them?

Woman They're such . . . pearly things.

Man Go on.

Woman I could get a spoon and prise it in your eye sockets.
This part here. Above the cheekbone. Your eyes would
water. Your tears would fill my spoon. So that when your

eyes eventually pop out they would land in the spoon with a gentle . . . splosh. Like the sound of a goldfish turning suddenly in its bowl.

Man   You're excelling yourself today.

Woman   Inspired by you, my muse.

Man   My snare.

Woman   My bayonet.

Man   My noose.

Woman   My hooligan.

Man   My ghost.

Pause.

Woman   Have you seen the view?

Slight pause.

Tell me, have you ever seen such a glorious day?

Man   Never.

Woman   Nor have I. And what about the sea? Have you ever seen it so clear and calm and tropically island perfect? In all the years we've been shipwrecked here.

Man   Shipwrecked?!

Woman   Yes. Stranded. Solitary. Have you ever seen the sky so blue and the sea so calm and the beach so smooth and the palm trees – oh, the palm trees! So full of coconuts and parrots and – Oh, look! Little monkeys! Hundreds of them! Thousands! Have you ever seen that? Well, have you, for fuck's sake? Ever?

Man   No.

Woman   Shall I tell you what I'm going to do?

Man   Why not?

Woman   I'm going to strip naked and run down to the beach. I'm going to feel the sun on my skin and the sand between my toes. I'm going to spin round and round till I'm dizzy. Then I'm going to fall to the ground and roll over and over till my whole body is golden and crunchy with sand. Then . . . you know what I'll do?

Man   What?

Woman   I'll rush into the sea and let the surf splash me clean. Its frothiness will . . . it will fizz all over my skin. I'll lick my lips and taste its salty warmth. Then I'll collect some seashells from along the shore – those tiny bright blue ones with flecks of gold – and I'll decorate my hair with them. Then I'll make a necklace of sea urchins and pearls. Then I'll sit on a rock – that one over there! Shaped like a whale. You see? And then I'll let the monkeys feed me mango and passion fruit. And then . . . oh, then I'll lay back, calm and tranquil, and drift into a universe of dreams on the back of my luxurious leviathan.

Pause.

Man   Your cunt.

Woman   . . . What about it?

Man   It's such a . . . a . . .

Woman   Mmm?

Man   A precocious thing.

Woman   Oh, you're flirting with me now.

Man   I could squeeze a grenade up there.

Woman   I should hope you'd lubricate it first.

Man   Of course. What d'you think I am? A savage?

Woman   No.

Man   A telly evangelist?

Woman   Oh, no!

Man   A vegan?

Woman   You? Never!

Man   Thank you. Of course I'd lubricate the grenade first. Not only would I thoroughly lubricate the grenade but I would thoroughly lubricate your pussy first.

Woman   You spoil me.

Man   I'm a romantic at heart.

Woman   I'd forgotten.

Man   . . . I'd pull back the layers of your cunt like the leaves of an artichoke. Your cunt would get pinker and pinker the deeper I get. When I've reached the deepest, pinkest, tenderest part, so tender I can see tiny veins like red hairs throbbing, I'd press the tip of the grenade inside you and –

Woman   Do grenades have 'tips'?

Man   . . . The *end* of the grenade.

Woman   What 'end'?

Man   The end that is not the pin-pulling end. I'd push it into you. At first your cunt might react against such a cold alien thing inside you. Your cunt would try to spit me out. But I would push gently, gently, gently, coaxing your convulsing cunt into acceptance. The muscles would begin to relax, begin to welcome this man-made fist of metal, spitting would become sucking. I would push deeper, deeper, deeper, and, gradually, you would learn to love this gunpowder egg nestled dynamite in your womb.

Slight pause.

Woman   I remember . . . when I was seventeen –

Man   The pin's still showing.

Woman   Eh? What?

Man The pin of the grenade. It's still peeking from your pussy. It's like the beak of a clockwork cuckoo.

Woman Oh . . . I see.

Man Shall I tell you what I'm going to do?

Woman Why not?

Man I'm going to tweak the beak.

Woman Really?

Man Really.

Woman Well, I'm not sure I want you to do that.

Man Well, I'm not sure you being not sure is enough to stop me.

Woman Really?

Man Really.

Slight pause.

I tweak.

Slight pause.

I tweak.

Slight pause.

You're beginning to enjoy each beak tweak.

Woman I'm not.

Man You are. Tweak.

Woman Oh . . . I am.

Man You urge me on to ever more audacious tweaking.

Woman Tweak my beak!

Man Your nipples become hard.

Woman Oh, tweak, tweak.

Man   I can see your whole body convulsing as if a cattle prod were shooting volts of lightning up your anus.

Woman   Tweak!

Man   Tweak!

Woman   Tweak!

Man   I pull the pin.

Woman *continues to moan.*

She reaches orgasm as –

Man   BOOOM!

Pause.

Woman   I remember – when I was seventeen – I was invited to this party. It was an eighteenth birthday party but – oh, it was special. It was given for a friend of a friend. Janis, that was my friend, she'd left school the year before me and got a job in some gift shop down Roman Road and one of the girls in the shop – her dad had just come into a whole lot of money – a lottery win or inheritance we all supposed – and he said he wanted to give his daughter the biggest birthday bash East London had ever seen. Anyway, this girl from the shop invited Janis – who she'd become bestest friends with apparently, though Janis hadn't mentioned her once before this, not once, but that's Janis all over – and Janis asked this girl, 'Can I bring someone?' and this girl said, 'Of course.' and so Janis – as I really *was* her bestest friend – asked me.

Man   . . . You seen the – ?

Woman   Invites were sent out. The most amazing invites you've ever seen. The paper was all textured and yellow like old parchment. And the writing was all swirly and curly and – oh, oh, all round the edges. Gold leaf! It used to come off on your fingers when you held it too long.

Man   You seen the – ?

Woman   'Dress Elegant.' That's what it said on the invite.
So me and Janis decided to have a day trip up West to get
new outfits and stuff. I had a part-time job in a pet shop
down Mare Street so I had a bit of money saved up, thank
God. Oh, I really splashed out that day. New dress, new
shoes, new earrings, make-up. I even bought a bottle of
perfume that cost an arm and a leg called *Romance*.

Man   You seen the – ?

Woman   On the day of the party – Saturday the sixteenth
of August – I started to get ready at nine in the morning. I
went to the hairdressers and had all my highlights re-done.
I had my nails done too. That was a first for me. Then I
came home and put this deep-cleanse cucumber and tea
tree face mask on. You're supposed to leave it on for fifteen
minutes but I thought, 'What the hell!' and kept it on for
three hours. I ran a bath and emptied an entire bottle of
rose and lavender bubble-bath in it. I soaked for ages. Then
I went to my bedroom and started to put on my make-up.
The new lipstick – *Sunrise Kiss* – tasted of strawberries and
the new mascara made my eyelashes look so long. Too long
– that's what I thought at first. But it wasn't. It was perfect.
And then . . . then I put my new dress on. It was green and it
shimmered and sparkled. I looked at myself in the mirror on
the back of the wardrobe door. Oh! . . . I look so beautiful. I
can't believe it's me.

Pause.

Man   You seen the view?

Woman   Er . . . not recently, no.

Man   That tsunami did a lot of damage.

Woman   . . . I suspected it would.

Man   The beach – it's just a rubbish tip of washed-up stuff
now. Look at it all! A car and a lawn-mower and . . . oh,
there's a double bed. A tumble-drier with a dent on the top.
A motor bike. A rosewood jewellery box. A tin of condensed

milk. A dildo shaped like a dolphin from the lost city of Atlantis.

Woman   . . . It's amazing what a common-or-garden tsunami can throw up.

Man   Shall I tell you what I'm going to do?

Woman   Why not?

Man   I'm going to strip naked and go down there. I'm gonna dip my hands in oil and paint tribal markings all over my face and skin. I'll find an old chain used on a slave ship and I'll decorate it with sharks' teeth and seagull skulls and then I'll hang it round my neck. Then I'll find an old crash helmet – black with a blood-red streak on it – and then I'll find old gloves once used for welding and then I'll find old jackboots once used to kick some poor fucker's face in. And then – know what I'll do?

Woman   Can't possibly imagine.

Man   I'm going to cover my genitals with a thong made of seaweed and lobster claws. I'll find a fender from a juggernaut lorry and I'll sharpen it on a large rock – that rock shaped like a whale – I'll sharpen it to a razor-sharp finish and then I'll swish it through the air like a mighty sword, yelling, 'I AM KING OF THIS ISLAND!'

Woman   What about me?

Man   Eh?

Woman   The last I heard I was drifting into a universe of dreams on the back of –

Man   You're washed away!

Woman   Washed away?

Man   Forgotten.

Woman   The monkeys will remember me.

Man   No, they won't.

Woman   Monkeys!

Man   The monkeys don't give a monkeys about you. After
the tsunami had subsided – and you were two hundred miles
out at fucking sea somewhere – you know what they did?
Your precious monkeys? They led me to a rock – that one
over there! Shaped like a whale. You see? Then they offered
me – me! – mango and passion fruit. Very tasty. Then
they encouraged me to lay back and drift into a universe
of dreams – Something moves! Something beneath the
wreckage! The monkeys scarper and hide in the palm trees.
Televisions and torpedoes – everything tumbles this way
and that way as a huge monster, the size of three double-
decker buses – three! – clambers to its feet. Or should I say
. . . flippers. It's a sea serpent. Look at it! Green and covered
with barnacles and broken harpoons. It has a long tail and
neck. Its head is a cross between a horse and an eagle with a
large dollop of dog thrown in. Its teeth are huge and yellow.
Its breath smells of shipwrecks and long-sunk submarines.
The Serpent roars so loud the wreckage shifts and shakes
from one end of the island to the other. Then the Serpent
glares at me with eyes the colour of arterial blood. I feel no
fear. I do not know the word 'fear'. I stand on top of the
whale-shaped rock and I cry, 'Fuck off this instant or, by
the hairs on my chinny-chin-chin, I will chop your fucking
head off!' The Serpent goes to bite me! I jump off the rock.
CHOMP! Its massive jaws shut. It looks at me out of the
corner of its blood-red eye. I swing my mighty sword and –
SLASH! – I slit the eye open. Green jelly erupts from the eye
and splashes all over me. The Serpent roars out in pain and
throws its head back. RAAAHHH! I jump from television to
tumble-drier to cocktail cabinet and then – in one acrobatic
and daredevil leap – I'm up on the back of the monstrous
creature. Its skin is scaly and smooth and it's difficult to
get a grip. It's like climbing a mountain covered in ice. A
mountain that wants to shake you off. I stick my sword in
the serpent's scaly smoothness again and again. Blood leaks
from the wounds and crawls down the green body like

crimson snakes. The Serpent is bucking like a bronco now. Its tail lashing this way and that – WHOOSHH! It's trying to swot me away as if I'm a pesky fly. WHOOSHH! But I am no fly. I am a fearless warrior King and this is my island and I'll destroy anyone or anything that threatens my shores. 'DIE, SERPENT, DIE!' I strike at the neck of the beast. Green skin opens to reveal pink beneath. SLASH! Pink! SLASH! Pink! The Serpent is roaring and bucking louder and harder than ever. I start climbing up its neck. I feel its blood pulse and pump beneath me. I'm standing on top of the Serpent's head now. I lean over to blind its other eye when – A flick of its head and – WHEEE! I'm up in the air. I'm spinning. Spinning and falling. I see the huge mouth open below me like a dark pit and the next thing I know – CHOMP! I'm in the mouth. Its tongue is like wet shag-pile carpet. It smells so bad I can barely breathe. And then its mouth fills with vile sewage-saliva and it's muscles squeeze in all round me like a vicious car wash and – GULP! The Serpent is swallowing me –NOOO! I'm sliding down the wet chute of its windpipe – it's like a slide into a swimming pool and – SPLASH! I'm in the massive drain of its gut. It's dark. But chinks of light are getting in through the wounds my sword had made. I can make out the remains of an old pirate ship and the rotary blades from a Black Hawk helicopter. Unless I act quick I'll be digested in gastric juices and the Serpent will pronounce itself ruler of my kingdom. I climb up the mast of the old pirate ship. I can see the shape of the Serpent's rib cage above me. I thrust up with my sword. It's like digging a hole in a sky made of meat. DIG! DIG! I can hear the Serpent roar with pain but there is nothing it can do to stop me. I hack a hole big enough to leap up and pull myself in. Like getting into an attic without a ladder. I get a good grip with my jack boots and – HACK! HACK! I'm cutting my way up through the body of the serpent now. I snatch breath in tiny pockets of air. SPLASH! Blood washes all round me. I'm like a miner in a mine of flesh and blood. And I'm mining in the direction of something I can hear. Something I can hear and feel. BA-BOOM! BA-BOOM! The beating heart

of the monster. HACK! HACK! BA-BOOM! BA-BOOM!
HACK! SPLASH! BA-BOOM! HACK! And then I see it! The
heart! Big as a car! It pumps and pumps. I hold my breath
and swim through a pool of blood and – STAB! I puncture
the heart with my sword. The heart quivers. The Serpent
lets out a massive roar – so loud I fear my ear drums will
burst. And then the heart – BA-BOOM . . . Ba . . . boom . . .
ba . . . boo . . . ba . . . ba . . . Silence. The Serpent is dead.
YESSS! I hack and hack through flesh and bone again until
– Sunlight! – I emerge from the side of the slain Serpent.
I gulp in the salty fresh air. Then – CHOP! – I cut off the
Serpent's head and yell, 'SO PERISH ALL WHO DARE
THREATEN ME AND MY FUCKING KINGDOM!'

Pause.

Woman   Your cock.

Man   . . . What about it?

Woman   It's such a . . . perky thing. Know what I'm going
to do? Cut it off. I'll buy a length of copper wire from that
old hardware shop down Shoreditch High Street. You know
the one. And then I'll buy new garden shears from that
garden centre on the road to Dagenham. Where we bought
that Japanese tree that time. Remember? The one infected
with mutant ladybirds that nearly ate the whole garden. And
then . . . what would I do? Oh, yes! I wait for a Saturday
night when you're out drinking with your mates. I sit up in
bed reading one of those paperback romances I got from
the charity shop down Columbia Road. The bedside lamp
is on. I'm eating chocolate. A box of chocolate truffles. It's
nearly midnight. You should be home from the *The Snog and
the Slag* or whatever the fucking pub's called by now. What's
happened to you? Perhaps you're entertaining everyone
with one of your piss-head watch-me-I'm-a-superhero stunts
. . . Read . . . Truffle – The front door! I hear you stumble up
the stairs. Bathroom door. Pissing. Some of it actually goes in
the toilet. You don't flush. You don't put the toilet seat down.
You don't wash your hands. You burst into the bedroom.

You kick off your shoes. You lose your balance and stumble this way and that way. You struggle out of your clothes. You throw your slightly soiled boxer shorts in my face. You think it's funny. Which it's not. Or sexy. Which is just plain scary. You cough up a big wad of phlegm. You swish it round your mouth like a wine taster, chew it, then swallow. You fall onto the bed with such fucking force I nearly bounce up to the ceiling. You roll on top of me. Your breath stinks of beer and whisky. Your face is slimy with sweat. Your pores are large as bullet holes. There's a hard bit of snot up your nose like the head of a locust. There's bits of gristle and peanut stuck between your teeth. You burp in my face. Your tongue is so furry I could perm it. You try to stick your tongue in my mouth. I turn away. One of your hands is groping between my legs. There's a bit of dried whitlow that scratches me. I wince with discomfort but you don't notice. Then – BAHM! – I push you aside and – in one acrobatic and daredevil leap – I'm out of bed and opening the bedside cabinet drawer. I take out the copper wire and the garden shears and – before you have a chance to burp or fart or simply pass out – I tie your wrists and ankles to the four corners of the bed. You squirm a little. The copper wire digs into your skin. I climb onto the bed and kneel between your spreadeagled legs. Your cock is flaccid and sweaty. It's like a button mushroom in a Brillo pad. Your bollocks are saggy and there's a bit of toilet paper stuck to your foreskin. I open the garden shears and place one blade on either side of your genitals. You're whimpering now. I start to close the shears together. Drops of blood – like crimson pearls – blossom along the silver blades. I close the blades tighter . . . tighter . . . Blood is now flowing freely. It gushes down your thighs and soaks into the sheets and the mattress. The blades close! You're screaming. Your cock and balls are cut off. They look like the neck and giblets from one of those free-range chickens we get from that farmers' market in Spitalfields. I pick up your cock and balls. I take them to the bathroom. I flush them down the toilet.

Slight pause.

Man I see a child.

Woman No. Don't!

Man . . . She's over there. See her? She's four and a half years old. She's sitting at her mum's dressing table. She's opening her mum's rosewood jewellery box. Oh, she's just gasped at all the treasure inside. Did you hear it? She's picking up a pair of earrings. Gold hearts. She's holding them up to her ears and – She's seen me! 'What you up to, sweetheart? . . . They *are* pretty, yes. Your mum was wearing them when I first met her, you know . . . Eh? . . . In a garden . . . No, no, not *our* garden. A big garden. More like a park really – What's? . . . Do you *really* want to know? . . . *Really* really? . . . Okay . . . It was night and . . . well, I'm walking through this . . . wilderness – Eh? A wilderness means there's nothing there. No houses, no streets, nothing . . . That's right. I'm not in the garden yet . . . Well, keep listening and daddy will tell you. So . . . I'm walking through this wilderness. It's getting colder and darker by the second. I'm getting a little bit scared now. I whistle to keep my spirits up . . . What's that? Something's moving in the dark. "Who's there?" And then I see. It's not a person. It's an animal – Oh, don't be scared, sweetheart, it's not a scary animal. It looks like a . . . a horse . . . I *know* you like horses . . . A white horse . . . I *know* you like white horses. It's so beautiful. I take a step towards it. The horse twitches and snorts . . . Don't laugh! That's how it went. I step close . . . It's not a horse! It's a unicorn – That's a horse but with a horn sticking out of its forehead. Unicorns are magical creatures. Most people think they're just a myth. That they don't really exist. I used to think that too but – Look! A flesh and blood unicorn right in front of me. I can feel its breath on my face. I reach out and . . . Its neck. Warm and damp. I feel a vein pulsing with blood. "Hello, boy . . . What you doing here, eh?" The unicorn flicks its head. I know what it wants me to do – Can you guess? . . . Clever girl. I jump up on its back and –

Whoosh! The unicorn starts running. Galloping! Yee-hah!
I hold on to its mane for all I'm worth . . . Faster . . . Faster
. . . It jumps over a log. I nearly fall off. It splashes through
a stream. I get wet. It rushes between trees – A branch!
Missed! Yee-hah! And then . . . then the unicorn comes to a
halt. I see a figure standing in the dark . . . It looks like . . .
Yes! It's a woman. I jump off the unicorn and walk up to her.
She's wearing gold earrings shaped like hearts. She looks
at me and smiles. I look into her eyes. It's like gazing into a
universe. I see stars and dinosaurs and whales and skeletons
and spaceships. I reach out and touch her hand. She says,
"They say unicorns lead us to our true love. Do you think
that's true?" I say, "I *know* it's true." We kiss. And, as we kiss,
trees grow all around us. Magical trees full of magical lights.
It gets warmer. The sky clears and stars appear. Music fills
the air. I'm not in a wilderness anymore. I'm in a garden.'

Slight pause.

Woman   . . . Have you seen the view?

Man   What – ? Oh! Is that Serpent still rotting down there?

Woman   It finished rotting years ago.

Man   Really?

Woman   Oh, yes. A lot's happened since the last time
you looked. That's what you get for drinking yourself into
oblivion with beer.

Man   Beer?!

Woman   With whisky chasers.

Man   Hang on, hang on! Where did all this booze come
from I wonder?

Woman   You found it in the wreckage. Don't you
remember? Two crates of beer and one crate of whisky. Some
ship's lost cargo I suppose. You took it into the jungle for a
five-day bender. We – that's the monkeys and me – we found
you unconscious in a pool of piss and vomit and sucking

your thumb like a baby. I can honestly say it was the most revolting and degrading sight I have ever witnessed. I asked the monkeys to wash you clean but it was too nauseous a job even for them. I didn't press them. After all, they had far more important things to do for me.

Man   Like what?

Woman   Like clearing away all the tsunami wreckage to begin with. That double bed. The tumble-drier with a dent on the top. The yucca plant. Tin of condensed milk. Rosewood jewellery box. That dildo shaped like a dolphin from the lost city of Atlantis. Everything has either been buried or thrown back into the sea. And then . . . why, then I asked the monkeys to turn the gigantic Serpent bones into my palace.

Man   Your *palace*?

Woman   Looks a bit like the Taj Mahal, don't you think?

Man   Oh, I get it. You're Queen of the Island now.

Woman   Always have been.

Man   Hang on, hang on! Correct me if I'm wrong but – Queen or not – weren't you washed away by the tsunami?

Woman   That's right.

Man   What's more, I hear it dragged you forty fathoms below the sea. And – again, correct me if I'm wrong – I believe you got tangled in some fishing net and struggled to escape and you fucking couldn't.

Woman   A bit of a nuisance, I admit.

Man   Well, didn't you fucking *drown*?

Woman   I can breathe under water.

Man   Since fucking when?

Woman   Since forever. I am descended from the great sea god Neptune.

Man   Well, that's a bit of fucking luck.

Woman   I can hardly believe it.

Man   I can hardly believe it myself.

Woman   My great, great, great grandfather was a whale. That rock on the beach – the one I was on when the tsunami washed me away – that's his fossil.

Man   You never mentioned this before.

Woman   I don't like to boast about my incredible ancestors. If you look further along the beach – over there – you'll find a rock in the shape of a dolphin.

Man   A distant cousin?

Woman   How'd you guess? In fact, this island is where all my relations – from the titchiest terrapin to the largest leviathan – all come to die. If you drain the lagoon in the northern peninsular you'll find skeletons of a million mermaids going back to the dawn of time.

Man   Well, fuck me.

Woman   My poor great-great-great aunt on my mother's side barely made it here to die, you know. Oh, yes. She was over two thousand years old, bless her, and off the coast of Iceland – the cold water helped her blood pressure – when she felt a little flutter in her heart that she instinctively knew heralded the end. She started making her way to this island at once but, somewhere off the coast of Big Horn, she suffered a stroke that paralysed her down her left side. And then – oh, poor great-great-great-aunt – she had a heart attack off the Strait of Gibraltar. She'd given up all hope of getting here. And then – oh, the most amazing good fortune. An earthquake somewhere between the Dorset coast and the Galapagos Islands caused the most enormous tsunami – we were all convinced it was magicked by my distant cousin, the Good Witch of the Dead Sea – and this tsunami carried my poor dying aunt all the way here where she washed up with, amongst other things, a dildo in the shape of a dolphin from the lost city of Atlantis – Oh, my aunt was a Serpent, by the way.

Man   I'd guessed as much.

Woman   My aunt . . . oh, she was so ill and weak. Stroke. Heart attack. Two thousand years old – that's about a hundred and ten in human years. It took all her energy to struggle to her feet – I mean, flippers. And then . . . you know what happened?

Man   Er . . . I killed her?

Woman   Tie him up!

Man   What?

Woman   The monkeys are taking you prisoner.

Man   I'll smash their fucking skulls in.

Woman   There's too many, I'm afraid.

Man   There's not.

Woman   There is! And you've still got a hangover. Keep still! – Take him to the grotto under the mountain.

Man   How long are you going to keep me here?

Woman   For the rest of your life – Chain him to that rock! You will never see another living person for as long as you live. You will remain here – unloved, untouched, unkissed. Goodbye.

Pause.

Man   I remember – when I was eighteen – dad felt a pain in his spine. Just here. He was a minicab driver. The bloody job was always giving him little aches and stuff. Usually mum ran him a hot bath with Epsom salts and the next morning he'd be fine. But this time . . . this time the pain didn't go. It got worse. 'Go to the doctors, dad!' He wouldn't. One night we got a phone call from his minicab office. Dad had passed out in the toilets. They'd called an ambulance. We all rushed to the London Hospital and found him on this trolley in a corridor. He blamed it all on some dodgy kipper he'd had for breakfast. The doctors did some tests. It wasn't a kipper. It was cancer. They told dad he had a year if he had chemo. Six months if he didn't. Dad said he'd rather have six months feeling okay than twelve feeling like shit, thank you very much. We begged him to have the treatment but he was a stubborn old bastard when he wanted to be. 'Your sister's gonna be eighteen in August,' he said. 'Me and your mum – we've got some money put aside and we've decided we want to give her – give *all* of us – a party we'll all remember.'

Woman   . . . I've brought you some food.

Man   Eh? What?

Woman   Grotto! Food!

Man   Oh! I thought only your monkeys did that. 'Never see another living person for as long as you live.' Ain't that what you said?

Woman   I'm the Queen. I can change my mind.

Man   Played on your conscience, did I?

Woman   On the contrary. I haven't thought about you for seven years.

Man   Seven years!

Woman   Easy to lose track of time in this dark and airless grotto, I suppose – Fuck me, you've aged badly. You were like an athlete when we first met. Yes, yes, I can admit it now – now all my fizz for you has finally fizzled flat – there was a time when just the sight of the vein pulsing in your neck made me feel so giddy I feared I might faint. But now . . . all I can think of is cholesterol.

Man   It's difficult to keep fit when you're chained to a rock.

Woman   A braver man would have tried to escape.

Man I did try. Only once. I pulled the chain out of the rock
with one savage tug – Yesss! I run out of the grotto. A stone
tunnel. I stumble down it. My bare feet are cut by sharp bits
of rock. And then I see it – Sunlight! Freedom! Run towards
it. The light gets brighter and brighter. I hear the sound of
the sea. The air gets fresher and sweeter. Rock beneath my
feet turns to sand – Ahhh! So bright. Hurts my eyes. I fall
to my knees. The heat of the sun on my skin! Sand so soft.
Seagulls. I open my eyes . . . palm trees, parrots, a pure
blue sky – What's that? A figure. Someone's splashing in the
water . . . It's a woman. The one who imprisoned me. She's
naked. Sunlight sparkles on her skin. She's so beautiful. The
most beautiful thing I've ever seen. Why didn't I realise it
before? Look at her! I can't bear the thought of not being
on the same island as her. Even if it means being chained
to a rock in a dark and airless grotto. I don't care. I'd
rather be unhappy in her world than happy in another. I
turn round. I walk back into the tunnel. Sunlight becomes
darkness. Sound of surf fades. Sand turns to rock. I'm back
in my grotto. I put my chain back into the rock. I can pull
it out anytime, of course. But I don't. I stay. And I live with
the hope that, one day, she might think of me with a new
fondness and save me from this loneliness.

Woman   . . . I see a child.

Man   . . . Go on.

Slight pause.

Man Go on. Please.

Woman She's sitting at the kitchen table. She's drawing.
She's using the big wax crayons I bought her. She's
concentrating so hard. Her tongue's running across her top
lip the way it does – You know?

Man Yeah.

Woman 'What you doing there, sweetheart? . . . Oh, it's a
unicorn. Look how beautiful it is – What's that? . . . What did

dad tell you? . . . Yes, yes. That's all true. Every word . . . '
And she smiles at me and – Oh, that smile. It's like a . . . like
a sunrise. She is . . . all my prayers answered – Prayers! Ha!
Remember those? 'Keep us safe.' You were right to laugh.

Man   I never laughed.

Woman   Flying saucers! I should've believed in them. We
could've sat on those hilltops together. Watching the night
skies. At least people don't tell you it's all part of UFOs' plan
if you lose . . . if you lose everything – Hear that?

Man   What?

Woman   The explosion.

Man   No, no, there's nothing.

Woman   Don't fucking tell me it's all in my head again.

Man   It's alright, it's alright.

Woman   I can hear her screaming – There's no air! I can't
breathe!

Man   Shush, shush.

Woman   No! Don't touch me! If you touch me I'll – Just
don't! . . . My lungs are being crushed . . . Help me! . . .
Help me!

Man   It's the tsunami. It's just washed you off your rock.
Remember? You were drifting into a universe of dreams and
then – Whoosh! It pulls you two hundred miles out to sea.

Woman   It . . . pulls me.

Man   Yes. It drags you forty fathoms below.

Woman   . . . Forty fathoms.

Man   Yes. You're caught in a net.

Woman   It's like a . . . a . . .

Man   What?

Woman   A giant spider's web.

Man   If you struggle the net only gets tighter.

Woman   I'm going to drown.

Man   No. You are descended from the sea god Neptune.

Woman   That's right. My marine DNA kicks in.

Man   You breathe water.

Woman   Gentle currents – they soothe me like the warm breath of a lover.

Man   Barnacles stick to your legs and belly.

Woman   I feed on plankton . . . My skin turns green with algae . . . Things swim by . . . seahorses . . .

Man   And you're calm . . . so calm . . .

Woman   Yes . . . calm . . . (*singing*) Fade and float.
Float and fade.
The world
I knew
has gone,
has gone.
Don't try to save.
Don't send a boat.
I'm happy remote
in fade and float.

Man   You can't stay here.

Woman   Oh, I can.

Man   What about me?

Woman   Join me.

Man and **Woman**   (*singing*) Fade and float.
Float and fade.
The world
I knew

has gone,
has gone.
Don't try to save.
Don't send a boat.
I'm happy remote
in fade and float.

Man *stops singing*.

Woman (*singing*)	**Man** (*overlapping* **Woman**)
Fade and float.	No!
Float and fade.	Stop it!
The world	Look at you!
I knew	You're becoming a ghost.
has gone,	I won't let that happen.
has gone.	You hear me?
Don't try to save.	I won't!
Don't send a boat	
I'm happy remote	
in fade and float.	

Man   I'm here to rescue you!

Woman   What – ? No.

Man   I am your great-uncle, the great silver swordfish of the Saratoga Sea, and you will be rescued whether you like it or not – There! My sword has cut you free.

Woman   But I don't want to –

Man   Shut up! A strong current is already carrying you back to the surface.

Slight pause.

Surface! Come on, come on!

Woman   Water rushes in my ears.

Man   Barnacles are washed from your legs and thighs.

Woman   I erupt into sunlight.

Man   And then – something beneath you.

Woman   What?

Man   A giant turtle.

Woman   I sit on its emerald green shell.

Man   It carries you back to the island.

Woman   Monkeys gathering all round me. They're so happy to see me. 'Hello, my monkeys, hello.' Mango and passion fruit? Yes, please, I'd love some . . . Oh, I was wrong to stay tangled for so long. What a selfish fool I've been. I'm needed here. 'LISTEN, MY MONKEYS! I AM QUEEN OF THIS ISLAND AND I WILL RULE YOU WITH COMPASSION AND LOVE!'

Man   And I am the King.

Woman   I'm afraid you forfeited that right when you got pissed.

Man   I did not get pissed.

Woman   There are over five thousand simian witnesses who saw you go into the jungle with crates of beer and whisky.

Man   To hide it from the monkeys.

Woman   And drink it yourself.

Man   No. Listen. After I killed the Serpent the monkeys gathered round me and cheered. We cut the serpent into steak-sized chunks and feasted on its flesh.

Woman   You ate my great-great-great-aunt!?

Man   And very tasty she was too. Then me and the monkeys – we sang and danced round a blazing fire. Everything was jolly and good spirited. But I knew if they got their hands on the beer and whisky I might have a drunken rebellion on my hands. You know what monkeys are like. So I took the booze into the jungle and buried it in a secret place. I didn't touch a single drop.

Woman   So explain being found in a pile of piss and vomit. Eh? . . . Come on!

Man   Untie me and I'll tell you.

Woman   You're untied.

Man   I'm in the jungle. I'm burying the booze. I'm burying it near the lagoon. It's getting dark now. There! Booze all buried. Scatter some palms leaves on top to conceal the place – Hang on! What's that? A light in the sky. So bright I can barely look at it. Brighter and brighter – It's a UFO! A beam of light comes out of the alien craft and – Ahhh! I'm floating up. Away from the jungle. The island is getting smaller and smaller. The sound of surf and monkeys celebrating gets fainter and fainter . . . Up . . . up . . . up . . .

Slight pause.

I'm laying on my back . . . Bright light above . . . Cool and hard beneath . . . Like marble . . . A gentle drone. Like the hum of a fridge . . . I'm naked! How the fuck did that happen? What's going on? I try to sit up . . . oh, I'm so weak . . .

Woman   Try again.

Man   I'm in a vast room. A white, glowing room. The light seems to come from everywhere and nowhere. I'm on a . . . a sort of plinth. I swing my legs over the edge. I stand up. Then – Visshhh! A door opens. And . . . oh, God!

Woman   What?

Man   Something's walking into the room.

Woman   What?

Man   It's . . . it's about the size of a seven-year-old child. Its skin is pale. The creature's eyes are huge and jet black – No! A hint of blue. Like two aubergines. The alien – it has no nose . . . no ears . . . no hair . . . no belly button . . . no genitals . . . It's got a mouth, but it's tiny and . . . no lips . . .

It has three fingers on each hand. It smiles at me. I smile back. I can't help myself. I feel at peace somehow. It says something but I don't understand a word. Its language is just gurgles and squeaks like . . .

Woman   Like a dolphin.

Man   And then . . . oh, something very strange. I start to hear its gurgling and squeaking in my head. And then . . . the gurgles and squeaks – they start to become words. It was like a radio tuning itself. And – fuck! – I hear the alien speak. In my skull. 'Do not be afraid, 'O! Perfect human specimen. We will not harm you.' I try to think of an answer but – 'Do not try telepathic talking. It takes many years to perfect. Speak out loud in your own language. I will understand.' The creature walks over to a window and beckons me to join it. In my skull I hear the alien say, 'Have you seen the view?'

Slight pause.

Woman   I remember . . . I left my bedroom and walked down the stairs. Mum must've heard me cos she rushed out of the front room and she looked up at me and – oh, the telly was on in the front room and I don't know what the programme was but, all of a sudden, there was all this clapping and cheering and a sort of fanfare thing on the telly and it was like . . . it was like it was for me – you know? – like it was *me* who was being clapped and cheered and fanfared and there were tears in my mum's eyes and her bottom lip was all trembling and stuff and I said, 'Mum, if you start crying then I will too and all my mascara will run,' and we both laughed and she kissed me and said, 'My beautiful baby' and, of course, that made me get all waterworksy again and I would have burst into tears, I swear I would, but at that moment there was a beep from a car outside and mum said, 'Your carriage awaits,' and – oh, oh, have I told you this? – all the guests who didn't have a car – we all had a lift to take us to the party cos it was miles out, in the countryside almost, and I . . . I – where was I? – I kissed mum and I went outside and – a warm evening, summer, the sun was just

setting – and . . . and – There was this Rolls-Royce outside! I
kid you not! There were pink ribbons going from the front
of the bonnet to the top of the windscreen and – There's
Janis! In the back seat. She waved at me and then the driver
– the chauffeur – he opened the back door for me and
helped me in the car and – Me and Janis, we just laughed.
The cab drove off and Janis said, 'You look unbelievable
tonight.' And I said she did too though, truth told, she didn't
and I feel a right bitch saying it, I really do, but Janis she
was just . . . Fat! Okay? And I'm not saying fat people can't
look great when they're all dressed up cos they can but Janis
couldn't, not really, not just cos she was fat but cos she . . .
she sort of didn't know she was fat. You know? So she wore
clothes for slim people on a fat body and it just looked . . .
well, rubbish but – oh, I know this is gonna sound awful but
what the hell – I couldn't help feeling sort of pleased cos I
knew that when we walked in the party all eyes would be
on me and not Janis – Music! Playing in the car! Piano! All
tinkly with lots of violins in the background. I looked out of
the cab and – oh, it was the perfect soundtrack as the streets
passed by and then . . . and then – and it seemed like we'd
only been in the car a few minutes but it must've been more
like a hour, perhaps more – I hear Janis say, 'Oh, God,' and
I look where she was looking and – A mansion! All flooded
with light. And the cab pulls up outside and the driver gets
out and opens the door for us and he holds my hand. 'You'll
be the belle of the ball,' he says. He did! I swear! There's
some people standing nearby and they all look so smart
and elegant and then this waiter comes up – yes, a waiter,
I kid you not – and he has all these glasses of champagne
on a silver tray and me and Janis take one each and there's
real pieces of fruit – mandarin, I think – in my glass and I
think, Don't choke on that! And then Janis's friend rushes
up and she's wearing this pale lemon silk thing and she looks
lovely, there's no denying it, just lovely and she says, 'Enjoy
yourselves' and she thanks me for coming – can you believe
it? *She* thanks *me* – and me and Janis walk into this . . . this
mansion place and the walls are covered with all these old

paintings of posh people in fancy clothes and on horses and
– An orchestra! There's a real orchestra playing and there's a
man singing and he's wearing a white suit and there's a rose
in his lapel and – oh, I can't take it all in, I just can't. And
then I see Janis and she's over by the French windows and
she beckons me over and she says, 'Have you seen the view?'

Man   I see auroras shimmering.

Woman   I see trees with magical lights.

Man   Asteroids near the sirens of Titan.

Woman   Oh, smell of flowers!

Man   Andromeda.

Woman   Hyacinths.

Slight pause.

Man   'You must be wondering why you're here.' Yes, I
am. 'Let me explain . . . You see that galaxy shaped like a
unicorn.' Yes. 'That is where my people come from.' It's
beautiful. 'We are a peaceful civilization. We delight in
gazing at starlight and smelling flowers. We never raise
our voices. We never lose our temper. We never get drunk
and put our fist through a door.' You haven't really got a
fist. 'This is also true. And for a long time we thought this
was the perfect way to live. A civilization without a fist. But
now we realise . . . it is not perfect.' How do you mean? 'We
have been attacked by another race from another planet.
They attack us with things that go boom!' Bombs? 'In our
language we have no word for such things. We have never
had need of them. We call them Things That Go Boom.
My only child was one of the first to be killed by one of the
Things That Go Boom. It happened in your equivalent of
the school playground. The day it happened my cry of grief
was so powerful it created a black hole in the universe – You
see it? There. Next to our galaxy.' I see it, yes. 'It's sucking
everything into it, as you can see. Very soon our own galaxy
will disappear into this endless dark. Like a unicorn hurling

itself into a black whirlpool.' Fight back! Drop bombs on
them! 'We tried. We made many Things That Go Boom.'
The alien waves his three-fingered hand and a door slides
opens – Visshhh! Bombs! Rows and rows of silver, gleaming
bombs. Atom bombs. 'You are impressed I can tell.' I am.
You could destroy any enemy with this lot. 'We could . . .
but we can't.' Why? 'There is no aggression in our DNA.
Even if we were capable of making a fist we would never
be able to use it. This is where you come in.' Me? 'We have
been searching this universe – and any number of parallel
universes – for the perfect aggressive male specimen.'

Woman   Oh, no, no, don't tell me! You had to screw a
million female aliens to save an entire civilisation from
extinction.

Man   No!

Woman   What did you do? Zip up in your biker-leathers
and promise them a spin round the rings of Saturn?

Man   It wasn't like that.

Woman   It's *always* like that.

Man   I would never cheat on you.

Woman   Ha!

Man   All they did was pluck a hair from my head. They
could extract all my DNA information from that. Alien
fingers didn't even touch my skin. They said their next
generation of children would grow to be warriors. But that
still left a problem. They were defenceless till then. 'We have
built craft that can drop the Things That Go Boom.' The
alien waves his hand and another door slides open and –
Fuck me! It's a vast room! Bigger than Wembley Stadium.
A spaceship in the middle of it. 'Perhaps you would like to
fly this ship to our enemies' planet and bomb them for us.'
Yesss! The next thing I know – I'm in the spaceship. I'm
sitting at a control panel. There's a window in front of me.
I feel a buzzing in my head and – Fuck! I know how to fly

the fucker. A hatch in Wembley Stadium room opens. Space
and stars beyond. I launch the ship. Whoosh! I whizz round
comets and meteors. Yee-hah! There! The planet I need to
bomb is looming in front of me. It's one big mother-fucker.
I fly down into its atmosphere. I see a city below me. I drop
a bomb and – BOOM! The sky turns bright white. The ship
shakes. And then – a mushroom cloud! So big. So bright.
Like a vast blossoming tree made of smoke and sparks. I
imagine all those murdering alien fuckers frying at the
ferocious radioactive roots. Scream, you bastards! Scream
in fucking agony. I whoosh to another city. Yeeh-hah!
Bombs away. BOOM! Mushroom cloud. Die! Burn! Scream!
Whoosh! Bombs away! Yeeh-hah! Whoosh! Bombs! Burn!
Blister! Scream! Suffer! Whoosh! Bombs away! Yeeh-hah!
Whoosh! Bombs! No mercy! None! I want to crush your
skulls beneath my boots – I'm out of the ship now. Yes! I've
got a flamethrower in one hand and a machine gun in the
other. I'm killing everything I see! Die, mother-fuckers! Die,
you mother-fuckers! Die! Die!

Woman   Stop it, stop it!

Man   I want to fucking kill them!

Woman   You're making yourself ill.

Man   I have to do *something*.

Woman   Not this! Look at you.

Man   . . . Help me.

Woman   It's . . . it's the radiation.

Man   Radiation?

Woman   From the bombs.

Man   I'm not in protective clothing!

Woman   I'll help you back to your ship.

Man   It takes me back to the big Mother Ship.

Woman   The aliens give you something for radiation sickness.

Man   A pill.

Woman   'We need to get you back home.'

Man   Next thing I know – I'm back on the island.

Woman   You're vomiting and pissing and sucking your thumb.

Man   And then you find me. And you accuse me of getting drunk on beer and whisky. Oh, the injustice of it all! – Listen, monkeys! I am your rightful ruler.

Woman   They'll never follow you.

Man   The monkeys are gathering behind me.

Woman   Only half – Look! The others are gathering behind me.

Man   My ones chant my name.

Woman   My ones chant *my* name – I am your Queen, my monkeys!

Man   I'm not just your King, my monkeys! I am your Messiah.

Woman   Messiah!?

Man   I saved an entire fucking race! How more messianic can you get?

Woman   Do a miracle then!

Man   I don't do party tricks.

Woman   Well, I do – Watch this!

Man   What's happening?

Woman   Scary, eh?

Man   *What*, for fuck's sake?

Woman   The tail that's growing from the bottom of my spine. See it? My wonderful green tail – Your monkeys are looking very scared.

Man   Don't be, my monkeys. I am your Lord, Slayer of Serpents and Saver of Alien Civilisations. It will take more than a green tail to scare me.

Woman   Good. I've *got* more.

Man   More tails?

Woman   Tentacles! Sprouting from my sides. You see? Look how huge they are! See them – all swirling and curling in the air. Yes! I am part octopus on my father's side and I can summon up this subterranean DNA anytime I like.

Man   Well, that's fucking handy, ain't it.

Woman   Don't you mean 'tentically'?

Man   Humour in the face of defeat. I admire that.

Woman   I won't be the one defeated.

Man   Surrender now or you'll be ripped apart limb from limb.

Woman   Never! Surrender now or *you'll* be ripped apart limb by limb.

Man   Never!

Woman *and* **Man**   WAR!!!

Pause.

Man   I remember . . . I heard dad screaming in the middle of the night. I rushed to him. My sister was already there. Dad was twisting himself this way and that – It was like he was possessed. You know? Real horror-film stuff. Mum was giving him pain-killers. My sister went to get a hot-water bottle because, usually, if you pressed one against his back the pain would ease off. But tonight . . . the pain kept getting worse and worse. I remember . . . at one point, as

we were struggling with him on the bed, dad's eyes sort of
locked with mine and it was like . . . like gazing into a million
years of stuff.

Slight pause.

Dad was constantly on morphine after that. He'd been
resisting taking it too much cos he said it made him feel like
a zombie but now . . . well, there was no choice anymore.
Thank fuck for the party – that's what we all kept saying.
It gave us something else to think about. There was just so
much to fucking organise. You know what was so amazing?
The way everyone helped. I always knew dad was popular
but I never realised . . . – His mate Navin persuaded
someone he knew – someone he did some private chauffeur
work for, rich bloke, film producer or something – he
persuaded this bloke to let us have the party in one of
the houses he owned. This bloke said there were lots of
events there so there was already floodlights and bars and
cloakroom and stuff. And then another mate, Harry, he said
he could get all the booze for next to nothing and someone
else offered to pay for all the sandwiches and someone else
all the little canapé things and someone else all the fruit and
– oh, yeah, this bloke who manned the phones or something
at the cab office said that his brother sang on cruise ships
and he was available that night if we wanted some free
cabaret. And all the cabbies that knew dad – every single one
of them – they offered to be chauffeurs that night. Dad said,
'You see how good people can be?'

Slight pause.

The day of the party – me and my mates got there at seven
in the morning. We put fairy lights up in all the trees and
made sure all the floodlights were working and . . . people –
they seemed to appear out of nowhere to help. Didn't know
half of them. And vans full of food rolled up . . . bars were
filled with drinks . . . ribbons put up the stairs . . . vases of
flowers everywhere . . . – it all just . . . happened. You know?

Like in those films where someone waves a magic wand and
. . . Shazam!

Slight pause.

I had a room where I could get ready. I shaved so close my
chin turned red raw and I thought, Fuck! Shaving rash!
But half an hour under a scalding shower seemed to calm
it down. I cleaned my teeth till the gums bled and then
I gargled away a whole bottle of Fresh Mint mouthwash.
I rolled Alpine Spring deodorant under my arms and
then splashed so much *Eau Sauvage* everywhere I nearly
choked myself to death. My clothes were on hangers and all
wrapped in plastic – light-blue suit, silk tie. Dad had bought
me some silver cufflinks. They looked just right. You know?
I spent ages gelling my hair. There was a curly bit in the
front and it wouldn't behave itself but I kept gelling and
pressing, gelling and pressing and – There! Now, stay there,
you curly fucker! I put a red rose in my lapel. Then . . . then
I looked at myself in the mirror on the back of the bathroom
door . . . Fuck! I look like a film star. I can't believe it's me.

Woman   THIS ISLAND BELONGS TO ME!

Man   Eh?

Woman   One of my tentacles grabs your leg!

Man   Oh! I cut it with my sword.

Woman   Ahhh! Another tentacle grabs your arm.

Man   What arm?

Woman   The one holding the sword.

Man   Other hand takes sword – WHACK!

Woman   What've you done?

Man   Chopped off your tentacle round my leg.

Woman   No.

Man   Yes. Scream.

Woman   Ahhhhh!

Man   Chop off tentacle holding my arm.

Woman   Ahhhhh!

Man   Look! My monkeys are attacking your monkeys.

Woman   My monkeys are attacking your monkeys.

Man   My monkeys kill lots of your monkeys.

Woman   My monkeys kill more of your monkeys.

Man   The palace of bone! – I climb to the top!

Woman   My tentacles reach up for you.

Man   I jump from rib bone to rib bone.

Woman   I smash each bone as you jump.

Man   You're demolishing your precious palace.

Woman   Don't care – I'll catch you!

Man   No, you won't.

Woman   Yes, I will.

Man   Seaweed hanging from the final rib.

Woman   You grab it!

Man   SWIIINGG!

Woman   No!

Man   WHACK! – Another tentacle gone!

Woman   I've still got six left.

Man   Five!

Woman   . . . Five, then.

Man   The palace is falling all around us.

Woman   Bones thud to the ground.

Man   Jump – Miss them!

Woman   Jump.

Man   Jump.

Woman   Your monkeys are crushed.

Man   Your monkeys are crushed.

Woman   Your sweat sparkles on your skin.

Man   Your blood soaks into sand.

Woman   My tail pick up the leviathan rock – Throw!

Man   Missed! I aim my sword – Throw!

Woman   Missed.

Man   Sticks in a tree!

Woman   My tail grabs the tree – Pull!

Man   Uprooted.

Woman   Throw.

Man   Leap.

Woman   The tree crushes ten more of your monkeys.

Man   A root of the tree. It's pointed and sharp!

Woman   Don't rip it off!

Man   I rip it off!

Woman   Don't stab me!

Man   I stab you!

Woman   Where?

Man   Tentacle.

Woman   Ahhh!

Man   Pinned to the ground.

Woman   No!

Man   Yes. I get my sword.

Woman   I pull root out.

Man   No.

Woman   Yes.

Man   I rush into jungle.

Woman   I chase after you.

Man   Sword – cutting through jungle! Hack! Hack!

Woman   Tentacles – knocking down trees! Smash! Smash!

Man   I climb tree!

Woman   Smash! Smash!

Man   Jump on your back.

Woman   Throw you off.

Man   Land on tombs of ancient monkey ancestors.

Woman   Tentacles smash tombs.

Man   Slash! Another tentacle gone.

Woman   No!

Man   Four left.

Woman   Who's counting?

Man   Your blood – it's dripping on ancient monkey skulls.

Woman   Your sweat – it's dripping on ancient monkey skulls.

Man   I punch your fucking face.

Woman   I claw your fucking face.

Man   Punch.

Woman   Claw!

Man   Punch!

Woman   Kick!

Man   Punch!

Woman   Punch!

Man   Kick!

Woman   Claw!

Man   Surrender?

Woman   Never!

Man   Stab!

Woman   Claw.

Man   Kick.

Woman   Surrender.

Man   Never.

Woman   Smash!

Man   Hack!

Woman   Smash.

Man   Lagoon!

Woman   Where?

Man   There!

Woman   Smash!

Man   Dive!

Woman   Dive!

Man   Splash!

Woman   Splash!

Man   Stab.

Woman   Miss.

Man   Stab!

Woman   Lash!

Man   Ahhh!

Woman   Neck!

Man   Tentacle?

Woman   Yes.

Man   Ahhh!

Woman   Throat!

Man   Ahhh!

Woman   Choke!

Man   No!

Woman   Squeeze.

Man   Wheeze.

Woman   Wheezing.

Man   Squeezing.

Woman   Tighter.

Man   Gasp.

Woman   Tighter.

Man   Gasp.

Woman   Tighter.

Man   Crocodile!

Woman   What!?

Man   Crocodile!

Woman   Where?

Man   There!

Woman   No!

Man   Snap!

Woman   Jaws?

Man   Yes.

Woman   Me?

Man   Leg.

Woman   Ahhhh!

Man   Blood.

Woman   Bleeding.

Man   Snap!

Woman   Again?

Man   Deeper.

Woman   Ahhh!

Man   Free!

Woman   Me?

Man   Me!

Woman   No!

Man   Swim.

Woman   Stab!

Man   Crocodile?

Woman   Dead.

Man   Impossible!

Woman   Possible!

Man   Shore.

Woman   Already?

Man   Already.

Woman   Swim.

Man   Breathe.

Woman   Swim.

Man   Run!

Woman   Shore.

Man   Already?

Woman   Already.

Man   Faster.

Woman   Chase.

Man   Hack.

Woman   Smash.

Man   Look!

Woman   What?

Man   Grenade!

Woman   No!

Man   Pin!

Woman   Don't!

Man   Pull!

Woman   Run!

Man   Throw!

Woman   BOOM!

Man   . . . Dead?

Woman   No.

Man   Stab.

Woman   Lash!

Man   Hack!

Woman   Kick.

Man   Punch!

Woman   Wait.

Man   What?

Woman   Here!

Man   What?

Woman   Grenade!

Man   No.

Woman   Pin!

Man   Don't!

Woman   Pull!

Man   Run!

Woman   Throw!

Man   Boom.

Woman   . . . Dead?

Man   . . . No.

Woman   Grenade!

Man   Another?

Woman   Boom!

Man   Grenade!

Woman   Another?

Man   Boom!

Woman   Boom!

Man   Boom!

Woman   Boom!

Man   Boom!

Woman   Look!

Man   What?

Woman   Everywhere.

Man   Destroyed?

Woman   Ruined.

Man   No.

Woman   Yes. Just me.

Man   And me.

Woman   The last two.

Man   I've still got a grenade.

Woman   I haven't.

Man   You . . . you haven't?

Woman   You've got the last one.

Man   I have?

Woman   Throw it.

Man   What?

Woman   Kill me.

Man   But . . .

Woman   Pull the pin.

Man   No.

Woman   You already have.

Man   What?

Woman   You've pulled the pin.

Man   I haven't.

Woman   You have.

Man   I haven't.

Woman   Throw it! Quick!

Man   But I . . . I . . .

Woman   Throw it! Throw it!

Man   Splash!

Woman   You've thrown it in the sea?

Man   Yes.

Woman   I *knew* you'd do that!

Man   You did?

Woman   I've still got a grenade.

Man   But you said –

Woman   I lied.

Man   You can't.

Woman   I did. My four remaining tentacles are round your ankles and wrists.

Man   This ain't fair!

Woman   I know. My tentacles lift you high.

Man   Put me down!

Woman   You're spreadeagled against the sky. My tail – It's ripping your clothes off.

Man   No!

Woman   You're naked and helpless.

Man   I'm not.

Woman   You are! The tip of my tail picks up my grenade – Know what I'm going to do with it?

Man   Push it up my arse?

Woman   How did you guess?

Man   Just lucky I suppose.

Woman   I'm pushing it in.

Man   No lubrication?

Woman   None.

Man   Ahhh!

Woman   Deeper.

Man   Ahhh!

Woman   It's in!

Man   Don't tell me. The pin's still showing.

Woman   Do you know what it looks like?

Man   Er . . . the beak of clockwork cuckoo?

Woman   I'm going to tweak that beak.

Man   I thought you would.

Woman   Tweak.

Man   I'm beginning to enjoy it?

Woman   You're beginning to enjoy it!

Man   Oh, yesss!

Woman   Your cock becomes hard.

Man   Tweak! Tweak!

Woman   I pull the pin.

Man continues to moan.

He reaches orgasm as –

Woman   BOOOM!

Long pause.

Man   Hello.

Woman   . . . Hello.

Man   You enjoying the party?

Woman   Oh . . . yes.

Man   It's a beautiful garden.

Woman   Yes . . . it is.

Man   You've been out here for ages.

Woman   Have you been watching me?

Man   No . . . I just . . . – Smell those flowers!

Woman   Hyacinths.

Man   So that's what they are.

Slight pause.

Woman   It's like being in a film. Don't you think? The music from the party and . . . everything.

Man   . . . Yeah.

Slight pause.

Man   You like the statue?

Woman   What statue?

Man   The unicorn. There.

Woman   Oh. Yes.

Man   It's hundreds of years old.

Woman   Really?

Man   The garden used to be full of things like this apparently. One by one they've all gone. Broken. Stolen. There's a monkey tucked in those bushes over there. And on the edge of the lake – Out there! You see that big rock?

Woman   Yes.

Man   That's a whale.

Woman   Oh.

Man   And . . . oh, you can't make it out from here, but in the middle of the lake there's a big serpent.

Woman   I'd like to see that.

Man   It's a bit of a let down. Its head's been knocked off.

Woman   Oh, dear.

Man   It's quite a place, eh?

Woman   The most wonderful place I've ever seen – Is it yours?

Man   Mine? Oh, no, no.

Woman   You seem to know a lot about it.

Man   I just like knowing about things.

Woman   You've got explorer's DNA.

Man   Eh?

Woman   . . . It's in your blood. Exploring things.

Man   Explore everywhere, me. On the other side of that hill – guess what I found!

Woman   What?

Man   A little cave. It's called Prisoner's Grotto. I'll show you if you like.

Woman   It's miles away.

Man   I've got my bike.

Woman A *motor*bike?

Man Drove it all the way here – Whoosh! Fancy a spin?

Woman Not in this dress.

Man . . . I've explored the whole house too, you know. Oh, yes. There's a cabinet of curiosities at the top of the stairs. Did you see it?

Woman No.

Man It's amazing. Full of stuff from all over the world. There's a little booklet of all the things in it – Here! You see? . . . Hang on! More light over here.

Woman . . . Oh, there's lots and lots.

Man Yeah.

Woman What's that bird there?

Man It's a clockwork cuckoo. Its beak opens and its wings flap when you wind it up apparently. Looks stunning in the flesh.

Woman In the metal.

Man . . . What?

Woman It's made of metal not –

Man Right. Good. Ha, ha, ha.

Slight pause.

Woman Wow! A dolphin?

Man Yeah. A little statue of a dolphin. From Atlantis.

Woman I love dolphins. It says . . . oh, it's written so small – what did they use it for?

Man Nothing.

Woman Oh, let me see.

Man It just says they used it as . . . as a little statue.

Woman   They used to use a little statue as . . . a little statue.

Man   Yes.

Woman   . . . I like your cufflinks.

Man   Crocodiles. Their jaws move – Snap! Snap!

Woman   Oh, that's cute.

Man   Cute?

Woman   . . . Well, when I say cute, I mean . . .

Man   You're Janis's friend.

Woman   That's right.

Man   I saw you both arrive.

Woman   Do you know Janis?

Man   No. I've seen her. When I've picked my sister up from work.

Woman   Oh . . . you're the brother of the birthday girl.

Man   That's me.

Slight pause.

Woman   It must have been a lot of work.

Man   What?

Woman   Putting on a party like this.

Man   It was worth it.

Woman   Oh, yes. I can't imagine going to a party this beautiful ever again. Not even if I live to a hundred.

Man   We wanted it to be special.

Woman   Your sister's very lucky. All I got for my birthday was a box of chocolates and some tights.

Man   Surely your boyfriend bought you something nice.

Woman   I haven't got a boyfriend.

Slight pause.

Man   You see all the stars.

Woman   So many.

Man   There's not much light pollution out here. I saw a UFO once, you know.

Woman   Really?

Man   When I was a kid. We went on holiday. This caravan place on the Isle of Sheppey. I was on the beach one day with my dad. The weather was all drizzly so we were the only ones there. And then I saw it. A light in the sky. Hovering.

Woman   Did your dad see it too?

Man   Oh, yeah. He tried to take a photo but – Whoosh! It flew off before he had a chance.

Slight pause.

When's your birthday?

Woman   December the first.

Man   How old will you be?

Woman   Eighteen.

Man   Well! You can see this party as being a bit for you too. In advance.

Woman   Oh, no, no. I couldn't do that. It's your sister's night.

Slight pause.

How old are you?

Man   Nineteen.

Woman   I would've said twenty-one at least.

Man   I've always looked old for my age.

Woman   Really?

Man   Yeah. When I was fourteen I could get drinks in bars – no problem. I was shaving by fifteen, you know.

Woman   Is that young?

Man   It is when it's really thick stubble like mine.

Woman   Really?

Man   Yeah. My mum says, 'You're a manly man. You're not one of those pretty boys.'

Woman   I don't like pretty boys.

Slight pause.

It will change your life a lot, I suppose.

Man   What will?

Woman   Your dad coming into so much money.

Man   Money?

Woman   This party. Everything.

Man   Oh . . . I see.

Woman   I wouldn't know what I'd do if I suddenly got a lot of money. Well, I'd buy a big house for my mum, of course. And make sure she never has to work again. She works on the checkout in a supermarket. She gets terrible pains in her shoulder from having to lift tins of food and stuff.

Man   Repetitive strain injury.

Woman   That's it!

Man   My dad has it too. He's a minicab driver.

Woman   Well, at least he won't have to do that anymore. He can get a chauffeur to drive him around for the rest of his life and . . . Wh-what's wrong?

Man   . . . Nothing.

Woman   I've said something wrong, haven't I?

Man   It's not your fault. You didn't know.

Woman   . . . It's your dad . . . He's not well, is he.

Man   This party . . . It's a sort of . . . goodbye.

Slight pause.

Woman   I never really knew my dad. He left us when I was six. Mum caught him snogging some slag from Snaresbrook and threw him out. I think she thought he'd come back but . . . well, she must have thrown him further than she thought. He used to send me presents at Christmas. These earrings are from him.

Man   They're nice.

Woman   I think so. Mum still loves dad. She says she doesn't but . . . she does. She's got a photo of him on her dressing table. He's on a tropical beach somewhere. He's holding a guitar. He was in a band.

Man   What were they called?

Woman   *Taj Mahal.* You wouldn't have heard of them. He just did local pubs and things. He sends me songs he's written.

Man   What're they like?

Woman   A bit . . . folksy, I guess.

Man   Sing one.

Woman   Oh, I can't.

Man   Go on. Please.

Woman   . . . (*singing*) Fade and float.
  Float and fade.
  The world
  I knew
  has gone –

(*Stops singing*) Oh, I can't do it with the music from the party. It's distracting me.

Man   You've got a good voice.

Woman   I'm in the choir.

Man   At school?

Woman   Church.

Man   . . . It sounded a bit sad. Your dad's song.

Woman   It is. Lonely. It made me cry. Mum got annoyed. She said, 'If he misses you that much he can always book you a flight so you can visit.'

Man   He's never done that?

Woman   No.

Man   Then your mum's right.

Woman   I know, I know. And I don't really miss him as such. It's just that . . . well, sometimes it's like . . . oh, it don't matter.

Man   No. Tell me.

Woman   You won't understand.

Man   Try me.

Woman   . . . It's like I've got this other life. And in this life . . . well, dad never left us. And he sees me grow up and he picks me up from school and he takes me to the zoo and things.

Man   Dad things.

Woman   Exactly. Sometimes I wake up and in the middle of the night and I have to think – I mean, really, really think – what life is real. Is dad in the next room sleeping with mum? Or did he leave us years ago?

Man   I have that with dad. Is he really dying or . . . I won't
be able to cope when he goes. I know I won't. I'll have to say
something at his funeral. I won't be able to do it. My voice
won't work.

Slight pause.

Woman   Shall I tell you what my mum once told me? She
said that . . . well, children lose their parents. That's natural.
Sometimes it happens sooner than they like and in ways that
they don't want but it's still . . . it's still the natural order. And
so we can cope with it. The only thing that we cannot cope
with is when a parent loses a child. Only that is too much for
us. Only that can drive us into madness. Everything else . . .
somehow . . . we cope.

Slight pause.

Man   Wanna see me climb a tree? Don't need a ladder. Me
and my mates – we can climb anything.

Woman   You shouldn't.

Man   Why?

Woman   It's dangerous.

Man   Exactly. I'm going to join the army.

Woman   Why?

Man   I want to liberate oppressed cultures around the
world.

Woman   You want to blow things up.

Man   Yesss!

Woman   You might get yourself killed.

Man   I might get killed crossing the road.

Woman   That's a bloody stupid thing to say. You might
get killed crossing a road but you won't get blown up by
a hand grenade or something, will you. Haven't you seen

those soldiers coming back from wars with their legs blown off and their faces all . . . ? – How can you even contemplate something like that when your dad's ill. What must your poor mum think? The fear of losing a husband *and* a son. Remember what I said about coping. How can you put your mum through that. It's not fair. It's wicked. You've got to tell your mum you will never join the army. You've got to tell her before the end of the party. I mean it.

Man   Alright, alright.

Woman   Don't say 'alright' like that. Promise me.

Man   I promise. Cross my heart.

Woman   . . . Okay. Good.

Man   God! Your eyes.

Woman   Wh-what about them?

Man   They're such . . . sparkling things.

Slight pause.

Woman   Oh! I like this song.

Man   So do I.

Woman   What's it called?

Man   I . . . I forget now.

Woman   I like this bit – Listen!

Man   . . . Oh, yeah! That's great.

Woman   I prefer something with a slow beat like this.

Man   Me too.

Woman   I can't dance to all that fast stuff.

Man   But this . . .

Woman   Oh, yes . . .

Slight pause.

Man   Do you . . . want to?

Woman   Dance? Here?

Man   Why not?

Woman   I . . . I'm not very good.

Man   I bet I'm worse.

Slight pause.

Slowly, they approach each other.

Slight pause.

Tentatively, they reach out to hold each other.

Slight pause.

Awkwardly, they start to dance.

Gradually, though, they gain in confidence.

It's like they dance through the journey of their relationship.

By the time they stop dancing, they are kissing.

Pause.

Woman   We . . . we should be going back.

Man   Oh . . . yeah. Of course.

Woman   Be careful where you walk.

Man   Why?

Woman   There's dead monkeys everywhere.

Man   . . . Oh. I see.

Slight pause.

Woman   Your mouth.

Man   What about it?

Woman   It's such a . . . wet thing.

Slight pause.

I could squeeze a bullet between those lips. Point first. Press it between those rosebud lips. Prise it between your pearly whites. Gently. I wouldn't break a single tooth. Your tongue would feel something cold and hard. Taste of metal and gunpowder. There might even be a slight retching reflex. I'd wait a moment. I'd make calming, soothing noises. I'd be like a tree full of doves spreading my cooing branches around you. Then I'd continue pushing slowly, so slowly. You'd be quite calm by now. Your mouth would relax. You would accept this bullet in your palette. It would feel as natural as a pearl in the palm of an oyster.

Man   You're in a fucking poetic mood.

Woman   It's all your fault.

Man   Me?

Woman   You inspire me.

Man   Oh, my love.

Woman   . . . My love.

Appendix

Fade and Float*
Lyric by Philip Ridley

I don't want to feel
the sun on my skin.
I don't want to let
reality in.
I just want to fade
fathoms below
with shadows and silence
all I know.

I don't want to hear
the sound of a child.
I don't want to feel things
so cruel and wild.
I just want a world
where gravity's less
Oh, come tidal flow,
give me your caress.

Fade and float.
Float and fade.
The world
I knew
has gone,
has gone.
Don't try to save.
Don't send a boat.
I'm happy remote
in fade and float.

I don't want to feel
your touch on my skin.
I don't want the journey
of love to begin.
It travels to tears
and breaks me apart.
I'm safer with fade
and float in my heart.

Fade and float.
Float and fade.
The world
I knew
has gone,
has gone.
Don't try to save.
Don't send a boat.
I'm happy remote
in fade and float.

Fade and float.
Float and fade.
The world
I knew
has gone,
has gone.
Don't try to save.
Don't send a boat.
I'm happy remote
in fade and float.

Fade and float.
Float and fade.
The world
I knew
has gone
has gone.
Don't try to save.
Don't send a boat.
I'm happy remote
in fade and float.

Although only the chorus is sung in the play itself (starkly and unaccompanied), a complete song lyric was written. This can be set and used how each production sees fit.

*Separately, this lyric has also been developed into a full studio recording by the group **Dreamskin Cradle** (sung by **Mary Leay**) and is available as a download purchase on Amazon, iTunes and all other major download sites.*

Five poems from the performance sequence

LOVESONGS FOR EXTINCT CREATURES

by Philip Ridley

YOUR LOVE

Your love
is more startling
than a million goldfish,
more distracting
than a roomful of moths,
more bewitching
than grasshoppers
on a baby.

Or –
to put it
another way –
if I should
put my hand
in a bucket
and have it
severed by
a shark,
I would
merely say,
'Oh, fuck it!
Such a big fish
in such
a little bucket.'
For nothing
could surprise me
as much as
your love.

DARK SKY CRAVING

my lips the waiting firework
so silent unlit fuse lips
rarely sparked though cosmos yearning
as your lips the new torch burning
closer sulphur, partly parted,
oh, my petrol and vanilla
oh, my torchblood struck and tinder

now liponlip our countdown started
blasting me your glowing lifeline
fuel our systems smoulder ripple
vital skull sparks outward tingle
to my plotting gunpowder pocket
no more turnback race we onward
taste us holding through our orbit

roman candle me in furnace
yes, your skinfire prism flaring
all my systems now combusting
total lightspeed now exploding
downward coasting somewhere ocean
as I tremble scorch and splashdown
singed these lips but your dark sky craving.

THE SILVER HAT

Loving you
is like wearing
a silver hat.
Everywhere I go
people stop me
and ask, 'What's that
remarkable thing
on your head?'

I used to see
other people
wearing silver hats
but never thought
I'd be lucky enough
to get one.
I thought I was
destined to be
one of those
unhappy,
unhatted
people.
But now . . .

Now I visit friends
just to show them
how wonderful I look.
Last night,
for example,
I went to see
a silver hatted person
I hadn't seen for ages.
We spoke of many
hat-related topics.

On the way home
I passed your house
and, suddenly,

found myself
writing a note
and slipping it
under your door.

In the morning
you'll find a
piece of paper
on your doormat.
I wonder what
you'll think when
you read,
'Please!
Don't ever take
your hat
away.'

I'M WAITING TO BE KILLED

Your teeth are nine inch nails, my love.
You smell of something burnt, my love
There's petrol in your blood, my love.
There's napalm in your breath, my love.
There's land mines in your chest, my love.
Oh, squiggle 'n' squirm.
Throggle 'n' thrill.
I'm waiting
to be killed.

There's bullets in your spine, my love.
Gunpowder on your skin, my love.
Your grip is like a noose, my love.
Your tongue's a sparking fuse, my love.
Your sighs are mustard gas, my love.
Oh, squiggle 'n' squirm.
Throggle 'n' thrill.
I'm waiting
to be killed.

Sulphuric are your tears, my love
And venom drips from teeth, my love.
Your words are cluster bombs, my love.
Your hair is razor wire, my love.
Your cocktails, Molotov, my love.
Oh, squiggle 'n' squirm.
Throggle 'n' thrill.
I'm waiting
to be killed.

THE SEAMS

Your love
is a needle
and thread
that stitches me
into myself,
sews up my eyes,
mouth, ears, nose,
anus:
every orifice safe
and leakless.

Darling,
this embroidery
is camouflage,
not armour.
It helps me disappear
but does not protect.

One day,
I know,
your loving will stop
and I'll fall apart
at the seams.